believe

Written and Compiled by Dan Zadra & Kobi Yamada • Edited by Kristel Wills • Designed by Jessica Phoenix

COMPENDIUM™
INCORPORATED

live inspired.

ACKNOWLEDGEMENTS
These quotations were gathered lovingly but unscientifically over several years and/or were contributed by many friends or acquaintances. Some arrived—and survived in our files—on scraps of paper and may therefore be imperfectly worded or attributed. To the authors, contributors and original sources, our thanks, and where appropriate, our apologies. —The Editors

WITH SPECIAL THANKS TO
Jason Aldrich, Gerry Baird, Jay Baird, Neil Beaton, Josie Bissett, Jim and Alyssa Darragh & Family, Tom DesLongchamp, Marta and Kyle Drevniak, Rob Estes, Ryanne and Eric Francy, Michael and Leianne Flynn & Family, Sarah Forster, Jennifer Hurwitz, Heidi Jones, Carol Anne Kennedy, June Martin, Steve and Janet Potter & Family, Diane Roger, Kirsten and Garrett Sessions, Andrea Shirley, Lin Smith, Clarie Yam and Erik Lee, Heidi Yamada & Family, Justi and Tote Yamada & Family, Bob and Val Yamada, Kaz and Kristin Yamada & Family, Tai and Joy Yamada, Anne Zadra, August and Arline Zadra, and Gus and Rosie Zadra.

CREDITS
Written and Compiled by Dan Zadra & Kobi Yamada
Edited by Kristel Wills
Designed by Jessica Phoenix

ISBN: 978-1-932319-85-9

1st Printing. 50K 06 09   Printed in China

THE START OF SOMETHING GOOD

The start to a better world, or a better life, or a better future is simply our belief that it is possible. The thoughts in these pages are inspiring and affirming, especially in difficult times. They remind us that self-confidence can work wonders, but mutual confidence can work miracles. Perhaps Tiffany Loren Rowe says it best: No matter what kind of challenge lies before you, "if somebody believes in you, and you believe in your dream, it can happen."

Believe in fresh starts
and new beginnings.

The capacity for hope is the most significant fact of life. It provides human beings with a sense of destination and the energy to get started.

NORMAN COUSINS

Believe that opportunity is everywhere and all around you.

People will try to tell you that all the great opportunities have been snapped up. In reality, the world changes every second, blowing new opportunities in all directions, including yours.

KEN HAKUTA

Believe that the universe is friendly and life is on your side.

What is life for? It is for you.

ABRAHAM MASLOW

Believe you are a
once-in-all-history event.

Be faithful to that which exists
nowhere but in yourself.

ANDRÉ GIDE

Believe you are here for a reason.

Believe in something big.
Your life is worth a noble motive.

WALTER ANDERSON

Believe that nothing is too good to be true.

Let others lead small lives, but not you. Let others argue over small things, but not you. Let others cry over small hurts, but not you. Let others leave their future in someone else's hands, but not you.

JIM ROHN

Believe you must
take your chance.

Act boldly and unseen forces
will come to your aid.

DOROTHEA BRANDE

Believe when others might not.

To be nobody-but-yourself in a world which is doing its best, night and day, to make you everybody but yourself—means to fight the hardest battle which any human being can fight—and never stop fighting.

E.E. CUMMINGS

Believe that passion persuades.

...everything in life responds
to the song of the heart.

ERNEST HOLMES

Believe in doing great work.

The key is to trust your heart to move where your unique talents can flourish. This old world will really spin when work becomes a joyous expression of the soul.

AL SACHAROV

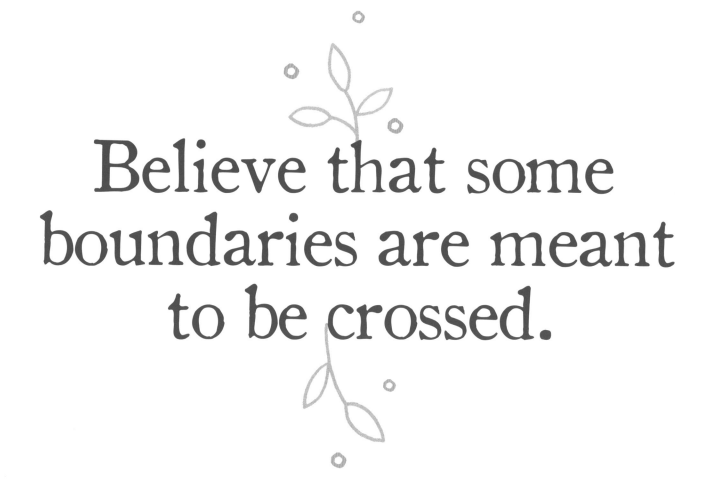

Believe that some boundaries are meant to be crossed.

Following the light of the sun,
we left the Old World.

CHRISTOPHER COLUMBUS

Believe there is always, always, always a way.

When you have exhausted all possibilities,
remember this: you haven't.

THOMAS EDISON

Believe you are far bigger than anything that can happen to you.

In your life's journey, there will be excitement and fulfillment, boredom and routine, and even the occasional train wreck.... But when you have picked a dream that is bigger than you personally, that truly reflects the ideals that you cherish, and that can positively affect others, then you will always have another reason for carrying on.

PAMELA MELROY

Believe there's light at the end of the tunnel.

Hope begins in the dark, the stubborn
hope that if you just show up and try to
do the right thing, the dawn will come.
You wait and watch and work;
you don't give up.

ANNE LAMOTT

Believe you might be that light for someone else.

You do build in darkness if you have faith. But one day the light returns and you discover that you have become a fortress which is impregnable to certain kinds of trouble; you may even find yourself needed and sought by others as a beacon in their dark.

OLGA ROSMANITH

Believe that
life is sacred.

Listen to your life. See it for the fathomless mystery that it is. ... Touch, taste, smell your way to the holy and hidden heart of it because in the last analysis all moments are key moments, and life itself is grace.

FREDERICK BUECHNER

Believe that the little things aren't little.

We can only be said to be alive in those moments when our hearts are conscious of our treasures.

THORNTON WILDER

Believe you are blessed.

The more you praise and celebrate your life,
the more there is in life to celebrate.

OPRAH WINFREY

Believe in the miracle
of the second chance.

The life you have led doesn't need
to be the only life you have.

ANNA QUINDLEN

Believe in giving back.

To enjoy the journey is to leap into people's lives. To enjoy the journey is to give until the stretch is a sacrifice. The question always is: what is it in life that will pull you out of your seat to be brave, risk and serve?

JANIE JASIN

Believe in love and everything it touches.

We all have the power to give away love, to love other people. And if we do so, we change the kind of person we are, and we change the kind of world we live in.

HAROLD KUSHNER

Believe the best about others.

You can work miracles by having faith in others. By choosing to think and believe the best about people, you are able to bring out the best in them.

BOB MOAWAD

Believe that friendship is an honor and privilege.

If you want trust, trust others.
If you want respect, respect others.
If you want help, help others. If you want
love and peace in your life, give them away.
If you want great friends, be one.
That's how it works.

DAN ZADRA

Believe in taking a stand.

You have to pick the places you
don't walk away from.

JOAN DIDION

Believe in doing the right thing because it's right.

Look the world straight in the eye.

HELEN KELLER

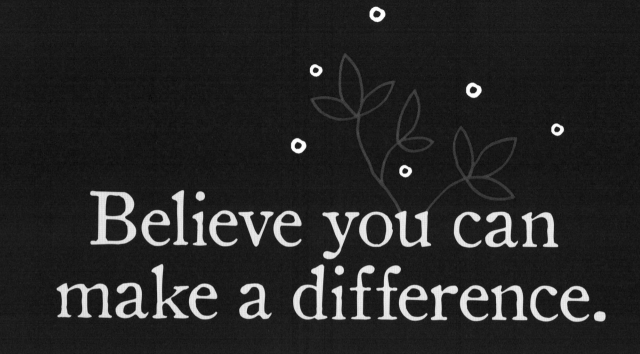

Believe you can
make a difference.

We won't always know whose lives we touched and made better for our having cared, because actions can sometimes have unforeseen ramifications. What's important is that you do care and you act.

CHARLOTTE LUNSFORD

Believe that together we are better.

What I do, you cannot do; but what you do,
I cannot do. The needs are great, and none
of us, including me, ever do great things.
But we can all do small things, with
great love, and together we can
do something wonderful.

MOTHER TERESA

Believe we can build
a better world.

How lovely to think that no one need wait a moment. We can start now, start slowly, changing the world. How lovely that everyone, great and small, can make a contribution toward introducing justice straightaway. And you can always, always give something, even if it is only kindness!

ANNE FRANK

Believe in today.

Life is a great and wondrous mystery, and the only thing we know that we have for sure is what is right here right now. Don't miss it.

LEO BUSCAGLIA

Believe that the best is yet to be.

Do not let your fire go out, spark by irreplaceable spark, in the hopeless swamps of the approximate, the not-quite, the not-yet, the not-at-all. Do not let the hero in your soul perish, in lonely frustration for the life you deserved, but have never been able to reach. Check your road and the nature of your battle. The world you desire can be won, it exists, it is real, it is possible, it is yours.

AYN RAND

Believe in yourself.